Short
Derbyshire &
the Peak District

Matthew Ross

COUNTRYSIDE BOOKS
NEWBURY BERKSHIRE

First published 2023
© 2023 Matthew Ross

COUNTRYSIDE BOOKS
3 Catherine Road
Newbury, Berkshire, RG14 7NA

To view our complete range of books please visit us at
www.countrysidebooks.co.uk

ISBN 978 1 84674 419 8

All materials used in the manufacture of this book carry FSC certification.

Produced by The Letterworks Ltd., Reading
Designed and Typeset by KT Designs, St Helens
Printed by Holywell Press, Oxford

Introduction

Derbyshire **has some of the most** diverse landscapes of any English county. It also represents a boundary, geographical and cultural, between the midlands and the north of England. From the fertile plains and former industrial heartlands of south Derbyshire, through the limestone dales of the White Peak, and finally to the rugged moorlands of Kinder and Bleaklow, the variety of terrain is staggering.

Of course, the Peak District gets the lion's share of attention. Iconic locations like Edale, Eyam and Monsal Head are rightly considered unmissable, and this book does not attempt to rock the boat in this regard. However, the further corners outside the national park have secrets and charm of their own. The National Forest, Moss Valley woodlands and Combs Valley are just some of the gems often bypassed by the traditional tourist itineraries.

In this volume, I have tried to incorporate both iconic and overlooked locations. I hope I have managed to throw a new light on some old favourites, and showcase some hidden gems too. If you're new to Derbyshire, the selection of walks should give you a good overall flavour of the county. If you're a seasoned veteran of these parts, then hopefully you will find some new routes from familiar locations, and some new locations

to uncover. I have made plenty of discoveries of my own while researching and writing these walks!

Each of the walks is between 1 ½ and 4 miles long: perfect for combining with a pub lunch or a visit to one of Derbyshire's many attractions. They're also just the right length for a summer evening stroll. The shorter length certainly doesn't preclude adventure! As well as gentle woodland and waterside strolls, you'll also find mini-mountain climbs, stunning viewpoints, lush forests and deep gorges, all accessible in just a couple of hours.

One of the many joys of short walking is that there is no rush. Rather than route marches, these are strolls that enable you to sink into the landscape and take your time. Within the text, I've tried to encourage some mindful moments for the walker, chances to appreciate the scenery, wildlife and heritage of these beautiful landscapes. Take a moment here and there to relax from the hectic pace of life. I hope you enjoy exploring Derbyshire's varied and beautiful landscapes as much as I have.

The terrain of the walks varies, but good walking shoes or boots are a must. The maps in this book are a good guide, but I'd recommend also having the appropriate Ordnance Survey map – referenced in the text for each walk.

Matthew Ross

Publisher's Note

We hope that you obtain considerable enjoyment from this book; great care has been taken in its preparation. Although at the time of publication all routes followed public rights of way or permitted paths, diversion orders can be made and permissions withdrawn.

We cannot, of course, be held responsible for such diversion orders or any inaccuracies in the text which result from these or any other changes to the routes, nor any damage which might result from walkers trespassing on private property. We are anxious, though, that all the details covering the walks are kept up to date, and would therefore welcome information from readers which would be relevant to future editions.

The simple sketch maps that accompany the walks in this book are based on notes made by the author whilst surveying the routes on the ground. They are designed to show you how to reach the start and to point out the main features of the overall circuit, and they contain a progression of numbers that relate to the paragraphs of the text.

However, for the benefit of a proper map, we do recommend that you purchase the relevant Ordnance Survey sheet covering your walk. Ordnance Survey maps are widely available, especially through booksellers and local newsagents.

Bottoms Reservoir

1 The Longdendale Valley

3¾ miles (6 km)

Start: Padfield village, where parking bays are available next to Temple Street play area. **Postcode:** SK13 1EL.
Public Transport: The 393 bus runs between Padfield, Hadfield and Glossop. Regular trains from Manchester to Hadfield.
OS Map: OL1 The Peak District: Dark Peak Area. **Grid Ref:** SK030961.
Terrain: Good paths and tracks through fields and woodland, with some gentle ascent and descent.
Refreshments: Drinks and food available at The Peel's Arms.

HIGHLIGHTS

The Longdendale Valley offers the first taste of the Dark Peak as you leave the Greater Manchester conurbation behind. Though the north side of the valley is dominated by the busy Woodhead Road, the south side is a peaceful area of farmland, woodlands and reservoirs, with great views to the moors above. Our walk explores this underrated corner of Derbyshire, starting from the pretty little village of Padfield.

THE WALK

❶ From the parking area at Temple Street play area, follow the road uphill, passing The Peel's Arms to reach a T-junction.

5

Derbyshire & the Peak District

2 Turn right on Padfield Main Road. Very shortly afterwards, take a public footpath on the left which leads between two houses before heading across the fields. Follow this pleasant path for 400m as it follows the contour of the valley.

3 Just before a metal gate crosses the path, cross a stile on the left. Follow a grassy path down through a field to another stile.

4 Cross the stile, and immediately turn right to reach the Longdendale Trail. Turn right again, along the trail. *It's hard to imagine now, but until the 1980s, this was the course of a major electric railway main line connecting Manchester with Sheffield. With the decline of coal traffic, the railway was closed and has since been turned into a multi-user trail. It also forms part of the Transpennine Trail, a long-distance route from Liverpool to Hull.* Continue on the trail for 1 mile.

5 The trail passes under a bridge; about 100m later, reach a signpost. Turn left here to leave the trail, following the sign for 'TPT West'. Go through a gate, cross a minor road and keep straight ahead, on a rough track heading downhill through woodland. The track bends to the left to follow the edge of Valehouse Reservoir, before emerging from the trees by Valehouse Dam.

6 Turn right to follow the road across the dam, which separates Valehouse and Bottoms reservoirs. *These are two of the five Longdendale reservoirs constructed to supply clean water to Manchester's cholera-stricken Victorian slums. Stretching the length of the valley, they were once the longest chain of reservoirs in the world: an audacious feat by engineer John Bateman.* To your right there are now great views up the valley, with the heather-covered hills of Tintwistle Knarr and Peaknaze Moor looming above the water.

7 Immediately after crossing the dam, leave the road on a path to your left, signposted 'Bottoms Path'. Follow the path through a larch plantation to arrive at a junction with another path by a large shed. Turn left and follow the path along the shore of Bottoms Reservoir. Continue as it leaves the water's edge, and then bends to the right around the edge of a woodland.

8 Cross a small footbridge over a water channel, and then follow the path up steps to meet a wide track. Turn left, heading downhill.

9 At the bottom of the hill, turn left to reach Bottoms Dam. On your right you will see an impressive outflow and gauging basin. After heavy rain this turns into an impressive fountain, another piece of Bateman ingenuity. Keep left on the higher of two paths crossing the dam.

Holybank Quarry (disused)

Valehouse Reservoir

Valehouse Farm

Tintwistle

Bottoms Reservoir

Longdendale Trail

Longdendale Valley

Padfield Main Road

The Peel's Arms

Padfield START

10 At the far side of the dam, turn left to follow the path along the edge of the reservoir.

11 Go through a gap in the wall to meet another path. Turn left and continue for 200m. Go through a gate on your right to take a field path signposted 'TPT East'. Head uphill to a gate visible among trees.

12 Go through the gate, under the old railway bridge and go straight ahead across the stile. Now follow your outward route across the fields to Padfield.

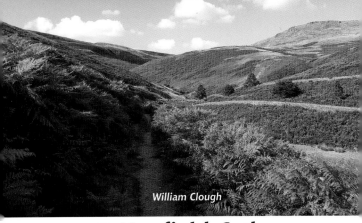

William Clough

2 Hayfield & the Kinder Trespass

4 miles (6.4 km)

Start: Bowden Bridge Car Park (pay & display), a short distance out of Hayfield on Kinder Road. **Postcode:** SK22 2LH.
Public Transport: 358 Stockport to Hayfield bus, 61 Buxton to Glossop bus.
OS Map: OL1 The Peak District: Dark Peak Area. **Grid Ref:** SK048869.
Terrain: Rough moorland paths with some steep ascent and descent.
Refreshments: The Sportsman Inn is 500m from the car park. There are also numerous pubs and cafés in Hayfield.

HIGHLIGHTS

Looming high above the surrounding countryside, the Kinder Scout plateau is the highest, wildest point in Derbyshire. Until relatively recently, access to the entire mountain was forbidden, and it became a pivotal location in the battle for the right to the roam the hills. This walk explores the western slopes, scene of the Kinder Mass Trespass in 1932. The views along the way, over Kinder Reservoir to the awe-inspiring bulk of the plateau, are superb. They are perhaps at their best in August, when the heather turns the hills pink and purple.

THE WALK

1 Begin at Bowden Bridge car park. This former quarry is the place where the Kinder Mass Trespass began, on 24 April 1932. From the entrance to the car park, cross the road and then go over the minor road bridge straight ahead. Immediately afterwards, turn right on the campsite entrance road. As you reach the campsite buildings, continue straight ahead on the footpath beside the river.

2 Continue along the riverside path for 500m, ignoring the first bridge over the river. Next to some houses, there is a second bridge over the river. Cross the bridge here and follow the path up to the road, emerging opposite the Sportsman Inn.

3 Turn left along Kinder road, continuing for 300m.

4 Turn right to leave the road at a public bridleway signpost. There is a plaque here, commemorating the arrest of the trespassers. Follow the bridleway uphill, through a series of gates and across fields for 1 mile. It's a steady climb, but there are great views down over Hayfield village. Be aware that there may be cows in these fields, so dogs will need to be kept on a lead.

5 A final gate leads out of the fields and onto moorland. Follow the path, called 'The Snake Path' straight ahead, through the heather. You will soon get your first views of Kinder, which dominates the skyline. In the other direction there are far-reaching views across Manchester and the Cheshire plain to the hills of North Wales. Continue for 500m to an old signpost, just in front of a gleaming white shooting cabin.

6 Turn right at the signpost, in the direction of 'Edale & Jacob's Ladder'. *You might also note the antiquated sign warning 'DO NOT TRESPASS!'. This is a reminder that, only 100 years ago, most of the beautiful landscapes around you were forbidden pleasures. The Kinder Trespass wasn't the first or only such protest, but it was instrumental in leading to improved footpath access, and ultimately the freedom to roam these moors which was granted in 2000.*

7 At a fork in the path, keep right to follow the bridleway sign, and continue down to a junction by a signpost and a gate.

Derbyshire & the Peak District

8 Leave the bridleway before it goes through the gate, instead following the path straight ahead, which curves around the hillside. Kinder Reservoir is now below you. Continue on the path as it follows a fence.

9 As the path curves away from the fence, there is a fork. Keep right to follow a rough path down into William Clough below. Some care is needed on this steep descent.

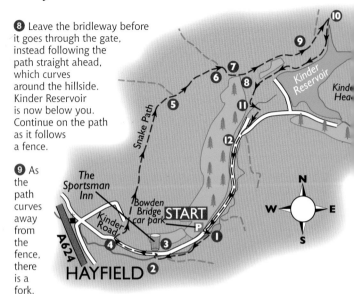

10 At the bottom of the hill, just before crossing a footbridge, turn sharp right. Follow this footpath which hugs the bank of the reservoir. Ignore turnings which head to the right, and continue until you reach the end of the reservoir.

11 Keep on the path beside the wall as it descends steeply to reach the reservoir access road. Turn left to take the path through rhododendrons and across a footbridge. Then turn right to follow the stream on the footpath.

12 Continue straight ahead when the footpath joins a lane. Follow the lane for 500m to return to Bowden Bridge.

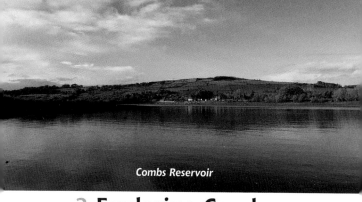

Combs Reservoir

3 Exploring Combs

2½ miles (4 km)

Start: Combs Reservoir car park (free). Alternatively, you may park at the Beehive Inn in Combs village, situated halfway along this walk. **Postcode:** SK23 9UN. There is also limited parking available in Combs village, so it is possible to start this walk at the Beehive, or to just do the short waterside walk between points 6 and 8, avoiding the hilly parts of the route.

Public Transport: The 199 Skyline bus passes Combs reservoir. Hourly trains between Buxton and Manchester call at Chapel-en-le-Frith station, about a mile's walk from Combs village.

OS Map: OL24 The Peak District: White Peak Area. **Grid Ref:** SK033797.

Terrain: Paths and quiet lanes through farmland and by water. One short, steep climb.

Refreshments: The Beehive pub in Combs is a terrific place to eat and drink, and also has a small shop on the premises, selling local produce.

HIGHLIGHTS

The valley of Combs is a hidden Derbyshire gem. Clustered beneath rugged moorland edges and set in a sea of meadows, its sandstone cottages and farms give off a timeless rural atmosphere. This walk combines a trip to the village with tranquil waterside views of Combs Reservoir and a climb up the hillside to appreciate fantastic views across the wider landscape of fields, hills, and moorlands.

Derbyshire & the Peak District

THE WALK

1 From the car park at Combs Reservoir, turn right on a quiet lane heading uphill. The lane crosses the railway line, and climbs gradually upwards towards the buildings at Meveril Farm.

2 As the lane ends among the buildings, there is a signpost indicating four paths, next to a ladder stile. Turn left here, through the gate to Tunstead Farm, then immediately keep right of the buildings on a grassy path heading slightly uphill. Go over a stile and continue on the path as it climbs steadily upwards beside a wall.

3 Ignore a turning to the left as the wall bends away, and keep on the path heading uphill. It's a steady climb, but your effort is rewarded with terrific views over Combs Reservoir to Chapel-en-le-Frith and Kinder Scout.

4 The climb finishes as you reach a gap stile in a wall. Cross it and turn left on a track. Soon you begin a gradual descent towards Combs village. Above the village you can also see the impressive crags of Castle Naze, where there are remains of a hillfort. Continue descending the track to reach a junction with a lane.

5 Turn left on this quiet lane, which winds downwards through fields and farms to reach the pretty little village of Combs. As you reach a road junction, the Beehive Inn is on your left. This is a fantastic place to stop for refreshment, and also features a small shop selling fresh produce such as vegetables, cheese and locally made oatcakes.

Eccles Pike

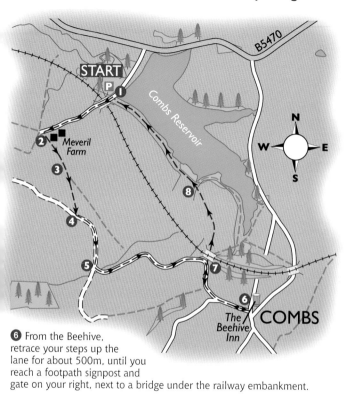

6 From the Beehive, retrace your steps up the lane for about 500m, until you reach a footpath signpost and gate on your right, next to a bridge under the railway embankment.

7 Take the path here to head under the railway line, and follow it across the fields. Cross a small wooden bridge over a stream, and turn left on the path running between the stream and Combs Reservoir.

8 Continue along this path, enjoying the views across the reservoir, to return to the dam and car park.

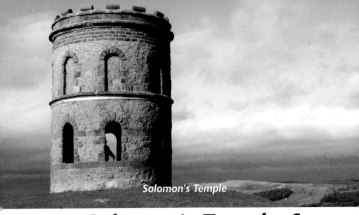

Solomon's Temple

4 Solomon's Temple & Buxton Country Park

1½ miles (2.2 km)

Start: Poole's Cavern Car Park (pay and display, toilets available).
    Postcode: SK17 9DH.
OS Map: OL24 The Peak District: White Peak Area. **Grid Ref:** SK050725.
Terrain: Good paths and tracks through woodland and grassland. Steady
    but gentle ascent and descent. Cows graze around the temple, so keep
    dogs on a lead.
Refreshments: Café at the Cavern is open during the day.

HIGHLIGHTS

Buxton Country Park is a delightful area of woodland, opening up on to
meadowland with wonderful views of the Dark and White Peaks. The whole
area is crowned by Solomon's Temple, also known as Grinlow Tower, a
castellated folly visible for miles around. This walk meanders through Grin
Low Woods before climbing upwards to the temple and back again. A great
walk for families, it can be combined with a trip to the Poole's Cavern show
cave or the Go Ape course for a full day out!

THE WALK

❶ From Café at the Cavern, turn right to follow the path around the edge of the car park. At the information board, turn right to enter the wood. Continue straight ahead up some steps.

2 The steps lead to a wide path. Turn left on the path, signposted for 'Solomon's Temple and Grinlow'. Immediately afterwards, the path splits. Keep right to follow the yellow waymarked path heading uphill.

3 Pass the sculpture of 'Charlie the Limeburner', a representation of the workers who once toiled in these woods, quarrying lime and preparing it in kilns. About 100m after the sculpture, keep right at a fork and continue heading uphill through the trees. At another junction, keep straight ahead to follow the sign to Solomon's Temple.

4 As you emerge from the trees at the top of the hill, turn left in front of a drystone wall to follow a grassy path through a clearing. This abandoned quarry working is a beautiful wildflower meadow in summer, full of flowers like orchids, harebells and the rare Grass of Parnassus. Keep on the path as it leads around the top of the old quarry, then keep right to leave the area by a gate.

5 The gate leads you onto the common land of Grin Low. Pass a bench to join a stony path heading to the left. You should now see the Solomon's Temple folly ahead of you; choose any route across the grassy land to reach it. *The temple was built in 1896 on the site of both a previous tower and a Bronze Age barrow. A spiral staircase inside gives access to a viewing platform, where there are great views over the surrounding countryside. To the north, Buxton spreads out below, with Combs Moss behind it, and Kinder Scout in the distance. To the south, the terrain is all rolling limestone hills, with the Staffordshire moorlands to the west. The contrasting scenery is a good reminder of the Peak District's different geologies.*

6 Once you have taken in the view, head straight downhill from the entrance to the temple to go through a gap in a wall. Keep straight ahead, descending through the hummocky remains of mining. Ignore a gate on your left, instead continuing downhill, crossing a ruined drystone wall. Keep to the left of a concrete pond, and follow the wall to a gate leading back into the woodland.

7 Go through the gate and fork left on a path. Immediately afterwards, reach a junction of small paths; continue straight down the hill.

Derbyshire & the Peak District

8 Arrive at another junction, next to a sculpture of a moon-gazing hare. Turn left and continue along this obvious path as it follows through the woods. There are a number of other sculptures along the way, celebrating the wildlife to be found in the woods. Continue for 500m until you meet another path.

9 Turn right, heading past the Go Ape course until you see some steps on your right. Go down the steps and follow the path back to the car park.

Café
START
P

Go Ape

BUXTON COUNTRY PARK

9

3

4   **5**

Grin Low

6

SOLOMON'S TEMPLE

8

7

N
W   E
S

5 Edale & the Nab

2½ miles (4 km)

Start: Edale Car Park. Pay and display – please be aware that the machines accept coins only, although cashback is available from the Penny Pot café. **Postcode:** S33 7ZQ.

Public Transport: Hourly trains along the Hope Valley line from Manchester to Sheffield.

OS Map: OL1 The Peak District: Dark Peak Area. **Grid Ref:** SK124853.

Terrain: Farm tracks and moorland paths, rough in places, with a steady climb.

Refreshments: The Rambler Inn and the Old Nag's Head pubs both provide hearty meals for walkers.

HIGHLIGHTS

In a tranquil green valley beneath the dark bulk of Kinder Scout, the village of Edale is one of the most iconic and popular Peak District spots. It is the start of the Pennine Way and many adventurous walks over the Kinder plateau. For those wanting something a little less strenuous, this short walk over the Nab still offers a taste of Edale's wilder side. A miniature climb of one of Kinder's foothills, it offers superb views across this special landscape.

Derbyshire & the Peak District

THE WALK

❶ Leave the car park by the exit next to the public toilets, and turn right along the lane. Continue straight ahead at the road junction, under the railway bridge and past the Rambler Inn. Follow the road through the village for 500m, passing the Edale Moorland Centre and charming village church to reach the Old Nag's Head pub.

❷ The Nag's Head marks the start of the Pennine Way, a 243-mile journey to the Scottish border. Assuming that you're not feeling quite so ambitious, continue straight ahead past the pub, following the sign for Grindsbrook. Shortly afterwards, the road turns into a tarmac track. Continue for 100m.

❸ At a set of white metal gates the track becomes a private driveway. Here you must leave the track and take a footpath on the right, signposted for Grindsbrook. Follow this path down a set of stone steps to cross Grinds Brook on a small wooden bridge. Ascend the stone steps on the other side of the stream and follow the stone flagged path into the fields of Grindsbrook meadows.

❹ Immediately after a small stone building, veer right on a broad grassy path across the field, which passes an old stone gate post and climbs up the hillside to the trees of Heardman's Plantation. The path is initially faint, but becomes much more obvious as it ascends to a gate.

❺ Go through the gate, and follow the stone-stepped path as it bends round to the right, climbing alongside the trees of the plantation. You gain height quickly as the path zig-zags up the side of the Nab, and there are now great views down into the Grindsbrook valley and the rocky edges of Kinder. Continue on the obvious stone path to climb through a switchback bend, to reach a junction of paths, and a flat, grassy area on your right. This is the mini summit known as the Nab. Pause here to enjoy wonderful views. The pointy hills of Win Hill and Lose Hill are visible to the east, and Mam Tor is directly opposite, while Edale village twinkles below.

❻ Once you've taken in the view, return to the junction of paths. Do not climb any further up the stone path, instead taking a grassy path on the right, which heads gently downwards. Follow the path through banks of heather and bilberry as it descends to the valley of Ollerbrook, bending right to run parallel with the stream.

7 Keep the stream on your left, and continue downhill through a gate to join a grassy farm track. Carry on through a series of gates to reach a cluster of buildings and lane at Ollerbrook Farm. Go through a gate, and immediately turn right through the farm buildings. Keep to the far left of the farmyard, to exit through a gate.

8 Continue on this farm track through two fields; exit by a gate, cross Grindsbrook on a bridge and meet a junction with the road. Turn left and retrace your outward journey back to the car park.

Grinds Brook

Oller Brook

6

5

THE NAB

7

Heardman's Plantation

4

The Old Nag's Head

3

N

W

E

S

Ollerbrook Farm

2

8

†

EDALE

The Rambler Inn

Edale Station

P START

1

6 Castleton's Caverns & Castle

3 miles (5 km)

Start: Castleton Car and Coach Park. There is a pay and display car park, but if you are early enough, there is free roadside parking along the main road. **Postcode:** S33 8WN.
Public Transport: The 272 Sheffield - Castleton bus runs roughly hourly, connecting with trains at Hope station.
OS Map: OL1 The Peak District: Dark Peak Area. **Grid Ref:** SK149830.
Terrain: Grassy paths and quiet lanes, with gentle ascent and descent.
Refreshments: There are many pubs and cafés in Castleton, including The Castle and Tilly's of Castleton.

HIGHLIGHTS

One of the most popular tourist destinations in the Peak District, Castleton sits in an impressive landscape of contrasting geology. Great sandstone hills rise to the north, while the south of the valley features deep limestone gorges. Caves, mines and Peveril Castle add plenty of historic interest too.

While the most celebrated walk from Castleton is the longer circuit of Mam Tor, this gentle route offers plenty of pleasures. In a short circuit of the wide, green valley, you are still able to see many of the main highlights, and enjoy great 360 degree views over the whole scene.

THE WALK

① From the entrance to the car park, cross the main road just to the right of the mini roundabout. Continue straight ahead between a shop and café, and then follow the public footpath to the left. This runs beside a pretty stream before meeting a road.

2 Turn right on the road, which crosses the stream, then climbs upwards between cottages. When the road ends and becomes a rough track, continue along it, following the sign for Speedwell Cavern.

3 Go through a gate and into fields. Keep on the path alongside the wall, as it curves around the valley side.

4 Go through a gate and cross the main road, which heads through the great limestone gorge of Winnats Pass to your left. (You might want to take a closer look at this before continuing; you can also find Speedwell Cavern here, which offers underground boat tours!) After crossing the road, continue straight ahead through a gap in the wall, signposted for Treak Cliff Cavern. This path splits almost immediately; keep right to go through a gap in a wall, and across a field to meet another road.

5 Turn left on this quiet road, and continue for just over ½ mile, passing Treak Cliff Cavern on your left. *200m past Treak Cliff, look for an unusual circular construction on the right, complete with a large millstone. This is a crushing circle, once used for crushing rocks and extracting lead. On the other side of the road, you can see the Odin Mine, where the rocks were mined.*

6 Continue on the road, to the point where a gate blocks it to traffic. This was once the main road to Manchester, but Mam Tor's constant landslips finally closed it in 1979. 'The Broken Road' now makes an unconventional but most enjoyable footpath; go through the gate to continue along it. You will soon see fabulous views over Castleton and right down the Hope Valley.

Derbyshire & the Peak District

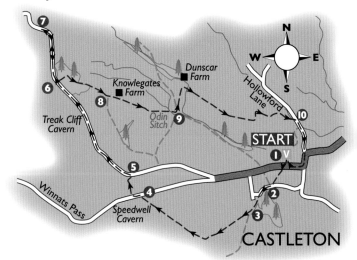

7 When you reach a bend where the old road lanes reduce from two to one, turn around. Retrace your steps to the crushing circle, and leave the road by the path on the left. Pass to the left of the circle and follow the path downhill.

8 Some steps lead you down to Knowlegates Farm. Keep straight ahead passing the buildings, and follow the path through fields. Cross the stream, Odin Sitch, and follow the path to meet a farm track.

9 Turn left on the farm track towards Dunscar Farm; continue for 100m. Just before the farm, turn right, signposted for Castleton. Follow this path through the fields, with wonderful views of the valley. Continue through a gate as the track turns into a walled track, meandering its way to meet Hollowford Lane.

10 Turn right on Hollowford Lane, which will lead you back to the main road in Castleton. Turn right at the junction, and follow the road around the bend, passing several cafés, shops and pubs. You will find the car park on your right.

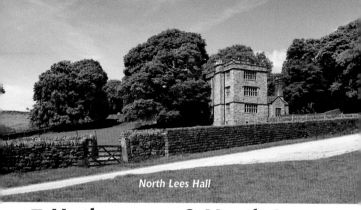

North Lees Hall

7 Hathersage & North Lees

4 miles (6.3 km)

Start: Oddfellows Road Car Park (pay & display). **Postcode:** S32 1DU.
Public Transport: Hourly mainline trains between Manchester &
Sheffield. The 272 Sheffield – Castleton bus and the 257 Sheffield –
Bakewell bus also pass through the village.
OS Map: OL1 The Peak District: Dark Peak Area. **Grid Ref:** SK231813.
Terrain: Tracks and paths through farms and woodland. Steady but
gentle ascent and descent.
Refreshments: Award-winning contemporary restaurant, Bank House in
Hathersage.

HIGHLIGHTS

The majestic gritstone edge of Stanage towers above Hathersage. The area
between the edge and the village is part of the North Lees Estate, an area of
meadows and moorland centred on North Lees Hall. This walk offers a tour
of the estate's lower reaches, passing wooded dells and historic ruins on the
way to the hall, with great views of Stanage and the valley below.

THE WALK

1 Leave the car park by the footpath at the bottom end, signposted for
'Toilets & Village'. Pass the Methodist church and arrive at the main road
through the village.

Derbyshire & the Peak District

2 Cross the road and turn right, passing Bank House restaurant. Just after a small car park, turn left along Baulk Lane. Pass cottages and allotments, then continue on this lovely waymarked track through a series of gates, the meadows ablaze with buttercups in early summer.

3 As you near a farm, follow the waymarkers on an obvious footpath that drops down to the left, avoiding the farm. Leave the field by a small gate and carry on along the path as it runs between a hedge and a small plantation. Continue past Brookfield Manor to reach a junction with Birley Lane.

4 Cross the road and continue straight ahead, through a gate and along a grassy path. Go through another small gate as the path enters woodland of oak, hazel and rowan, with a carpet of bluebells in spring. The path continues beside a lovely brook.

5 At a junction of paths next to a footbridge continue straight ahead on the same side of the brook, signposted for Stanage. Continue as the path rises through the trees, and then follows a fence along the edge of the woodland.

6 Arrive at a prominent stone marker with painted arrows on it, next to stepping stones across the stream. Our route is going to turn right here, but it's worth having a little explore around this area first. If you cross the stream, you will find a lovely glade for picnics, and the remains of an old millpond. When you've finished exploring, return to the stone post, and follow the path leading through a gate into a field.

7 Follow the path as it climbs uphill through pastureland. Pass through a gate and look for the remains of Holy Trinity chapel on your right. After another gate, descend gently towards a wooded valley, with Stanage above. Arriving at a gate, instead of entering the woods, double back on a path heading downhill.

8 Go through a gate to pass the distinctive hall at North Lees and follow the tarmac driveway downhill to meet a road.

9 Cross the road and follow the public footpath straight ahead. Shortly after, turn right on a farm track, then follow some prominent waymarks that guide you to leave the track on a path to the left.

10 Continue on the path as it passes above a farm and through a series of gates and fields; soon St Michael's Church appears in view. Join another path from the left and follow the hedge down to a stream.

11 Cross the stream on a small slab bridge and climb the bank on the other side. At the top, turn right on a path. Go through a gate and meet a lane; turn left and walk past the churchyard until you reach a lychgate on your right. Follow the public footpath into the churchyard; as you pass the church doorway, look out for the alleged grave of Robin Hood's companion Little John on the left! Continue ahead on the path to the bottom of the churchyard. Leave the churchyard by a gate and continue downhill to reach Baulk Lane.

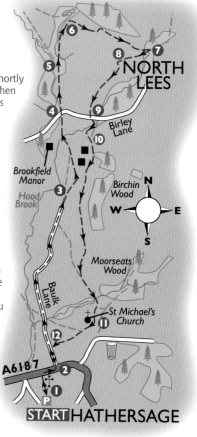

12 Turn left on the lane to return to the village and car park.

25

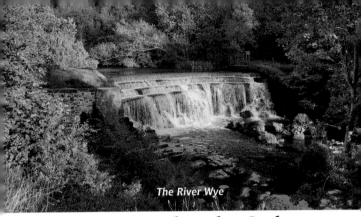

The River Wye

8 Monsal Dale & the River Wye

1¾ miles (2.5 km)

Start: Monsal Head Car Park. There are two pay & display car parks adjacent to the Monsal Head Hotel, a large one and a smaller one. **Postcode:** DE45 1NL.
Public Transport: The 173 Bakewell – Castleton bus (infrequent times).
OS Map: OL24 The Peak District: White Peak Area. **Grid Ref:** SK185714.
Terrain: Paths and trails through woods and alongside the river; rocky in places. The sides of the valley are steep, meaning that the ascent and descent are considerable – they're over reasonably quickly though!
Refreshments: Hobb's Café and Monsal Head Hotel & Bar are both adjacent to the car park.

HIGHLIGHTS

The old railway viaduct spanning the deep valley of Monsal Dale provides one of the Peak District's most iconic views. This walk offers different perspectives on the famous scene as you pass over, then under, the viaduct. Continuing beside the idyllic River Wye, your return journey takes you through peaceful woodlands. Monsal Dale is at its best in summer when the valley turns a deep green, sprinkled with wild flowers, but the views are spectacular at any time of year!

THE WALK

❶ Begin at the small car park at Monsal Head viewpoint. There is a pub here, as well as Hobb's Café & Craft Centre, and often an ice cream van. With the café behind you, head straight ahead to the viewpoint. Take a while to enjoy the magnificent sweep of scenery as the River Wye cuts through the limestone rocks. Once you've taken it all in, take the path to the right, signposted 'Upper Dale & Monsal Viaduct'.

❷ Continue down this stepped path to reach another signpost at a path junction. Turn left here, following the sign for 'Viaduct & Monsal Trail'.

❸ Continue down the path as it descends through hazel trees to reach the Monsal Trail. *This was the old Midland Railway main line from Manchester to London, opened in 1863 but closed in 1968. The line was well-engineered through the limestone contours, meaning that many tunnels and viaducts were necessary. Though these were closed to access for many years, the trail now runs through all of them.* On your left you can see the portal of Headstone Tunnel, but our walk turns right, to cross the viaduct. Enjoy more terrific views, down to the River Wye, and back up to the viewpoint you have descended from. Take a moment to stop and imagine steam trains thundering by on their way to London!

❹ Almost immediately after crossing the viaduct, reach a signpost. Turn right on the public bridleway to 'Monsal Head via Nether Dale'. Pass through a gate and descend gently to the valley bottom.

❺ The path leads you down to the River Wye. Turn right along the riverside path and continue beside the river, passing under the arches of the viaduct. You can really appreciate the scale of the construction from down here!

❻ After the viaduct, continue through a stone gap. There is a fork in the path here; keep left to remain beside the River Wye. This is a nature-rich environment, home to birds like dippers and goosanders, while high above on your left is the Iron Age hillfort of Fin Cop.

❼ Continue past an impressive weir. Shortly afterwards, you will see a metal footbridge on your left. Use this to cross the river, and then follow the path to the left as it heads back upstream.

Derbyshire & the Peak District

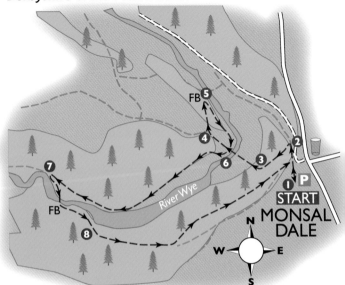

8 Pass the weir again, and continue on the path as it leads you through a gate and climbs steadily uphill through the woods. This is a great example of a limestone woodland, full of wild flowers like the pretty white stars of Wood Anemones. Continue on this path to return to the viewpoint. At the end of your climb, you've earned an ice cream!

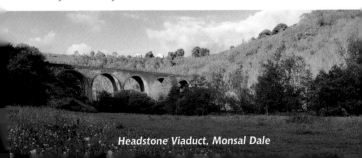

Headstone Viaduct, Monsal Dale

9 Longstone Edge

3 miles (5 km)

Start: The White Lion, Main Street, Great Longstone (free street parking available). **Postcode:** DE45 1TA.
Public Transport: The 173 Bakewell – Castleton bus, a few times a day.
OS Map: OL24 The Peak District: White Peak Area. **Grid Ref:** SK199717.
Terrain: Good paths, tracks and lanes across fields. One short ascent, but not too strenuous.
Refreshments: The family-run traditional White Lion in Great Longstone.

HIGHLIGHTS

Longstone Edge rises above the surrounding countryside, offering great views across the White Peak. It also boasts a rich flora and fauna, with birds, wild flowers and butterflies plentiful. This lovely route from the charming and unspoiled village of Great Longstone explores the fields and meadows below before traversing the Edge.

THE WALK

❶ Begin at the White Lion pub in Great Longstone, and walk up Church Lane, passing the lovely little church of St Giles. Not long after the lane bends to the right, turn left on a track, signposted 'Public Footpath'. Shortly afterwards, turn right along a walled footpath.

❷ As the walled track bends around to the left, go straight ahead through a gap in the wall to head across a field. Continue straight ahead as you pass through another gate and cross a concrete track, eventually reaching a set of stone steps over a drystone wall.

❸ Go over the steps and turn left along the walled track, Hardrake Lane. This old farm track is lined with wild flowers. In summertime, look out for butterflies among flowers like red campion, cranesbill and bedstraw.

❹ Follow the snaking path for 500m; it eventually opens out into a flowery area. Just after this, go through a gap next to a gate. Head straight on across a concrete slab track, heading for a green metal sign straight ahead. This signpost indicates a plethora of different paths! Turn directly left, signposted 'Longstone Edge', ascending gently up the field towards the ridge. Pass through a gap stile and go straight ahead, crossing stone steps over a wall to enter the access land of Longstone Edge.

❺ Follow the path to the left climbing through hawthorn trees. At a waymark post, veer slightly to the right as indicated and emerge from the scrub onto limestone grassland.

❻ The path rises to meet a track; turn left to immediately encounter a fork. Take the right-hand option here to climb further up the Edge, through gorse and hawthorn. As you reach the top of the Edge, the track bends. Cross a stile on your left, taking a path to the minor road over Longstone Edge.

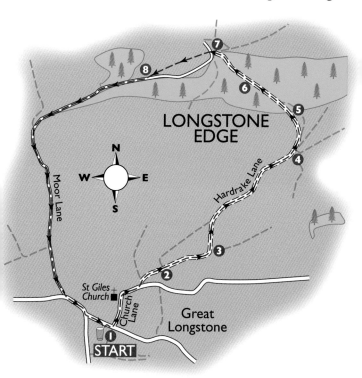

7 Cross the road and the stile to a grassy path running along the top of the Edge. Shortly after, take the left-hand fork in the path, descending slightly. This path heads down through the gorse to meet the minor road. Continue downhill on this quiet lane as it sweeps gently down the side of the Edge, offering terrific views towards Bakewell, Chatsworth and Monsal Head.

8 Keep descending the quiet lane for just over ½ mile, eventually reaching a junction with another road. Turn left to return to Great Longstone village.

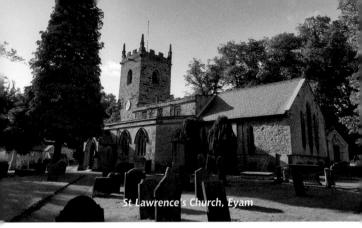

St Lawrence's Church, Eyam

10 Eyam

3¼ miles (5.5 km)

Start: Eyam Car Park, Hawkhill Road. There are two car parks here: one is free, but if you're feeling particularly munificent, there is also a council-run pay & display option. **Postcode:** S32 5AD.

Public Transport: The 65 Sheffield-Tideswell bus, with onward connections to/from Buxton.

OS Map: OL24 The Peak District: White Peak Area. **Grid Ref:** SK216767.

Terrain: Field paths, lanes and tracks, with steady ascent and descent.

Refreshments: The Moon Inn, Stoney Middleton, offers traditional pub fayre made from freshly prepared, locally sourced ingredients.

HIGHLIGHTS

Eyam is famed as 'The Plague Village', and a wealth of history from this era is still in evidence, from quaint cottages to 17th-century gravestones, poignant reminders of the losses suffered. This circular walk links Eyam with its lesser-known neighbour Stoney Middleton, which has interesting features of its own, including a fine pub, The Moon Inn.

THE WALK

❶ From the car park, turn left to descend to a T-junction. Turn left again to follow Church Street through the village. *There is plenty of historical interest*

32

as you pass the village stocks, Eyam Hall and church. Just after the church is the house which belonged to tailor Alexander Hadfield; the plague apparently arrived in Eyam in a parcel of cloth delivered here.

2 Reaching a fork in the road, keep left to arrive in the village square. Continue straight ahead, passing the tea rooms, and follow New Road as it rises out of the village.

3 Just after the last houses, reach a fork in the road. Take the left fork, Riley Lane, heading gently uphill. Climb steadily through woodland for 300m; emerging from the trees, bear right at another fork, on the lane signed for Top Riley. Pass the Riley Graves on your left. *Fear of spreading the plague meant that families had to bury their own dead in un-consecrated graves like these.*

4 At a signpost reading 'Byway Open To All Traffic', leave the lane, bearing right to follow this rough track through beech woodland. Shortly afterwards, reach a crossing of paths. Turn right, following the signposted footpath downhill. As the path descends through fields, there are wonderful views across the Derwent Valley to Curbar Edge. Continue to reach a road.

5 Head straight across the road to a walled track heading downhill to the right, signposted 'Public Footpath'. This track is a little rough underfoot, so take care. A graveyard on the left heralds your arrival in Stoney Middleton, and the track becomes a tarmac lane shortly after. Continue past the 'Roman' Bath House on your right. *Though not actually Roman, this has existed here for several hundred years, and was once a local attraction for health tourists. Apparently, the waters were beneficial for curing rheumatism and "saltness of blood". I'd recommend slaking your thirst at The Moon Inn instead, though…*

6 Continue along the lane, passing the unusual church of St Martin. *Its octagonal nave is one of only two in the country, and it's well worth popping inside for a look.* The lane meets the main road; cross it to reach The Moon Inn.

7 Once refreshed, re-cross the road, and begin retracing your steps along The Nook. Almost immediately, there is a junction; turn left to head uphill between cottages.

8 Just before the lane starts to head back down towards the main road,

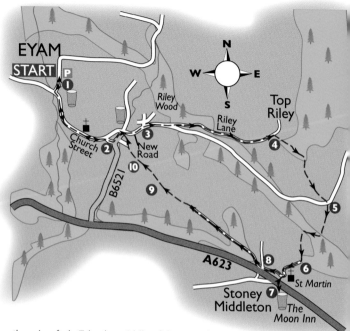

there is a fork. Take the middle of three roads
to follow Cliff Bottom uphill, passing a chapel on your right. The lane curves
past a small quarry now used for parking; immediately afterwards, leave
the road through a gate on the left, and follow the grassy path uphill.

9 Just after cresting the hill, pass Eyam Boundary Stone. *During their
quarantine, villagers left coins here to pay for goods delivered from neighbouring
villages. They soaked the coins in vinegar, believing that this killed germs; the
acidic effect of the vinegar left circular indentions still visible in the rock.*

10 The path leaves the fields through a gap stile, and eventually joins a
lane. Continue downhill past the Lydgate Graves to return to Eyam centre.
Turn left on the road, and retrace your outward route to the car park.

11 Troway & the Moss Valley Woodlands

3 miles (4.5 km)

Start: The centre of Troway hamlet, next to The Gate Inn and Troway Hall. There is road parking available here. **Postcode:** S21 5RU.
OS Map: Explorer 278 Sheffield & Barnsley. **Grid Ref:** SK386797.
Terrain: Good paths and tracks through fields and woodland, with some ascent and descent.
Refreshments: The Beestro café at Troway Hall is open during the daytime Tuesday – Sunday and has a lovely outdoor seating area, plus a shop selling honey products. The Gate Inn serves drinks and meals.

HIGHLIGHTS

Despite its proximity to both Dronfield and the outer reaches of Sheffield, the rolling valley of The Moss remains a hidden gem. The pretty hamlet of Troway is our starting point for a walk offering big skies, rolling cornfields and lush green woodland, with fabulous displays of bluebells and wild garlic in springtime.

THE WALK

1 From Troway Hall, turn right on the road. At the bend in the road opposite The Gate Inn, look for a public footpath sign. Take this footpath, initially between a wall and a hedge, and follow it across a stile into a field.

Derbyshire & the Peak District

Continue along the top of the field, and then cross another stile to go into woodland. Follow the path through the trees to a footbridge over a stream.

2 After crossing the stream, leave the wood by a stile, then ascend steps to reach a farm track. Turn right, and head downhill to Sicklebrook Farm. Continue straight ahead past the farm buildings, keeping left to join a footpath next to a hedge. Continue for 500m to a junction of tracks.

3 Turn left on the tarmac bridleway, Owler Car Lane. Pass a small gas plant on your left, and continue straight ahead on the track for another 200m.

4 As the bridleway arrives at a wooded area, look for a track with a vehicle barrier on the right. Turn right on this track into Owler Car Wood. Almost immediately, leave the track on a path to the left. This initially keeps parallel with the track before heading downhill through lovely beech woodland; this area is carpeted with bluebells in spring. Keep on this path to the bottom of the hill, to a footbridge over a stream.

5 Cross the bridge and follow the path as it bends around to the left. Immediately afterwards, the path divides into three. Take the right-hand option, and then turn right again as you meet another footpath. There is a large fallen tree here, which provides a fantastic place to sit and indulge in a bit of 'forest bathing'. Listen for bird song and look out for birds like great spotted woodpeckers, great tits and nuthatches above you. Continue along the path, ignoring turnings to the left; after about 200m you arrive at a footbridge over a stream, The Moss.

6 Cross the bridge and follow the footpath as it bends to the right. At a waymarker post keep right, then go through a gap stile into a meadow

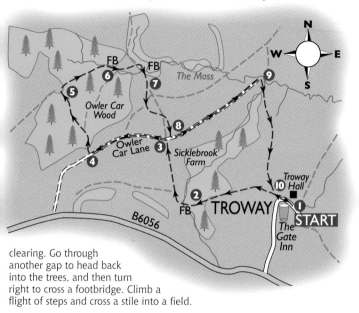

clearing. Go through
another gap to head back
into the trees, and then turn
right to cross a footbridge. Climb a
flight of steps and cross a stile into a field.

7 Follow the path straight through the field to reach a bench at the top. Turn left in front of the bench, and follow the path along the top of the field. Follow the waymarkers to cross another stile and head over one more field to reach a junction of tracks.

8 Turn left, on the tarmac bridleway heading gently downhill. Continue for ¾ mile, ignoring turnings until you reach a ford at the bottom of the hill.

9 Turn right just before the ford, and follow the path through trees, then around the edge of a field to a gap in the hedge on your right. Go through the gap and follow the obvious path uphill through two more fields.

10 At the top of the second field, go straight ahead over a stile, then turn left at the top of the field; return to Troway on this footpath.

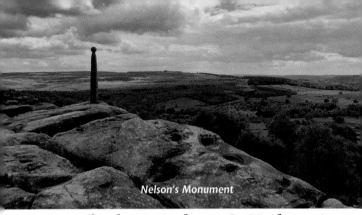

Nelson's Monument

12 Birchen Edge & Nelson's Monument

2 miles (3 km)

Start: Birchen Edge car park (pay and display), situated just off the A619, next to The Robin Hood Inn. **Postcode:** DE45 1PU.
Public Transport: The 170 Chesterfield – Bakewell bus.
OS Map: OL24 The Peak District: White Peak Area. **Grid Ref:** SK280721.
Terrain: Moorland and woodland. Slightly rough paths with one short, stiff climb.
Refreshments: Drinks, meals and snacks at The Robin Hood Inn. Also several pubs and cafés in nearby Baslow.

HIGHLIGHTS

The eastern moors of the Peak District culminate in some impressive, rocky edges. While Stanage, Curbar and Burbage Edges are popular hotspots, Birchen Edge remains something of a hidden gem. Rising out of enchanting birch woodland, the rocky crags are crowned by some intriguing monuments dating from the Napoleonic wars.

THE WALK

❶ From the Birchen Edge/Robin Hood car park, turn left on the road, following the signpost for Birchen Edge. Pass the buildings of Robin Hood

Farm, and then take a path on the left, heading slightly uphill. Go through a gate and follow the path up steps into peaceful woodland of birch trees and bracken.

❷ After about 500m, reach a fork in the path; turn right to climb up onto the rocky Edge above you. Some care is needed on this section, which is quite steep and rocky underfoot, but it's only a short distance to reach the top and your effort will soon be repaid!

❸ Reaching the top of the climb, continue on the path as it follows Birchen Edge to the left. This is an open area of heather moorland, and there are now wonderful views over to Baslow and the rolling fields of the White Peak beyond. Keep on the path as it passes through an area of boulders; you will soon glimpse the distinctive, slender column of Nelson's Monument on the horizon. Continue on the path along the edge towards this, ignoring a small path heading down to the left.

❹ Reaching the monument, take a moment to pause and have a closer look. *There is an inscription on the column: "OCT 21 1805": the date of the Battle of Trafalgar. The monument was erected in 1810 by local patriot John Brightman. While it may not be as impressive as Nelson's Column in London, it pre-dates it by some thirty years!*

Close by you will notice three impressive boulders. Their prow-like shapes led them to be compared to Nelson's ships, and they were engraved with

Derbyshire & the Peak District

names accordingly: *DEFIANCE, VICTORY* and *ROYAL SOVERIN* (sic). Over two centuries later, the carved names remain.

5 That concludes our Military History lesson! Now, continue straight on past the monument until you reach a trig point. Immediately behind the trig point is a narrow path, heading downhill to the left. Carefully descend on this path until you reach a junction with another path, in front of a large boulder.

6 Turn left on this sandy trod, which leads along the bottom of the Edge. Ignore all turnings and continue on this obvious path as it weaves in and out of birch trees and bracken. From here you can look up to Birchen Edge from below and appreciate its rugged sandstone formations. Continue on the path to return to the road.

7 Turn right on the road to reach the car park and the Robin Hood Inn.

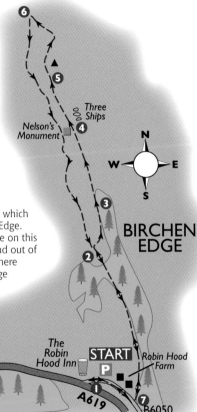

The River Derwent

13 Chatsworth & A River Ramble

2½ miles (4 km)

Start: Chatsworth House main car park. **Postcode:** DE45 1PP.
Public Transport: The 218 bus from Sheffield – Bakewell stops at Chatsworth hourly. In peak season, there are additional shuttles from Baslow village.
OS Map: OL24 The Peak District: White Peak Area. **Grid Ref:** SK261703.
Terrain: Easy-going paths by the river and over grassland.
Refreshments: The Cavendish & Flying Childers restaurants at the Chatsworth stable buildings serve meals. There is also a small cabin by the main car park offering ice creams, soft drinks and snacks.

HIGHLIGHTS

Home to the Duke and Duchess of Devonshire, the Chatsworth Estate is one of the most popular locations to visit in Derbyshire. With its smooth curves, placid river and clusters of lime trees, the elegant planned landscape offers a contrast to the wilder moorland edges above. This walk offers a gentle wander beside the River Derwent, heading back over the pastures via the enchantingly pretty village of Edensor. It makes a perfect accompaniment to a visit to Chatsworth House and gardens.

THE WALK

❶ From the stable buildings at the main car park, head downhill, keeping

Derbyshire & the Peak District

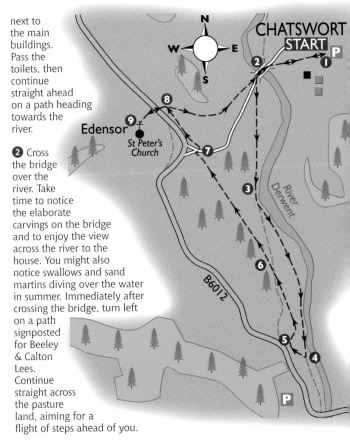

next to the main buildings. Pass the toilets, then continue straight ahead on a path heading towards the river.

2 Cross the bridge over the river. Take time to notice the elaborate carvings on the bridge and to enjoy the view across the river to the house. You might also notice swallows and sand martins diving over the water in summer. Immediately after crossing the bridge, turn left on a path signposted for Beeley & Calton Lees. Continue straight across the pasture land, aiming for a flight of steps ahead of you.

3 Climb the steps, then keep left to follow the riverbank, passing a weir. Keep a lookout for Chatsworth's herd of fallow deer grazing on the other side of the water. After another weir, arrive at the evocative ruins of an old mill.

❹ Just after passing the mill, turn right on a grassy path that heads slightly uphill and loops around the back of the ruins. Very shortly afterwards, arrive at a crossing with a well-defined dirt footpath.

❺ Turn right on this footpath. Cross a small stream then continue on the footpath, which runs along the edge of a grassy bank, elevated above the riverside. Keep on this path until you see the weir below you.

❻ Just after passing the weir, by a row of trees, keep left on a grassy trod heading away from the river. Initially the path keeps along the edge of the grassy bank, before dropping down to meet a lane.

❼ Turn right on the lane, then immediately turn left on a side track towards a cottage. The track ends at the cottage, but a grassy path continues ahead to meet the road in Edensor village.

❽ Cross the road and go through the impressive gates into Edensor village, a charming assortment of rose-wreathed cottages. St Peter's Church is straight ahead of you, and the Edensor village tearoom is just on the left.

❾ When you have finished exploring Edensor, retrace your steps through the gate, re-cross the road and continue on the obvious footpath, which begins next to a tree with a bench around it. This well-surfaced path leads you through lime trees to meet the Chatsworth entrance road just before the river bridge. Cross the bridge and return to the car park.

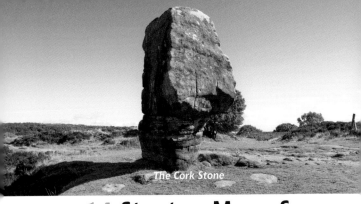

The Cork Stone

14 Stanton Moor & Nine Ladies

2½ miles (3.7 km)

> **Start:** The Red Lion Inn, Main Street, Birchover. Plenty of street parking.
>   **Postcode:** DE4 2BN.
> **Public Transport:** The 172 Bakewell – Matlock bus.
> **OS Map:** OL24 The Peak District: White Peak Area. **Grid Ref:** SK237621.
> **Terrain:** Moorland paths and quiet lanes. Some ascent and descent.
> **Refreshments:** The Red Lion Inn or the Druid Inn are both in Birchover
>   and have a good reputation with locals and visitors alike.

HIGHLIGHTS

Stanton Moor is a fascinating area of natural and human history. One of the most southerly areas of moorland in Derbyshire, it offers intriguing historic relics, as well as wonderful panoramic views. This route takes a southern approach to the moor, from the overlooked village of Birchover. There's also an optional extension to explore Rowtor Rocks and the Druid's Cave!

THE WALK

❶ From the Red Lion Inn, head uphill along the main street through Birchover.

❷ When you reach the last houses in the village, turn right on the tarmac track to Barn Farm Camping and caravan park.

❸ Just before the campsite buildings, leave the tarmac track to follow a public footpath signpost pointing straight ahead. Go through a gap in a wall, then immediately turn left on a grassy path around the back of Barn Farm, signposted for Stanton Moor.

❹ Pass between a large barn and a small cottage. Immediately afterwards, keep right, following a signposted footpath past the end of the campsite to reach a quiet lane.

❺ Turn right on the lane. Very soon afterwards, leave the road on a footpath to the left. Cross a stile to enter Stanton Moor.

❻ At a junction of paths, continue straight ahead to climb gently towards the top of the moor.

❼ Soon after, at a crossing of paths, turn right. There are now terrific views across to Matlock, with Riber Hall prominent on the skyline. Keep on this obvious sandy path through heather and bilberry, continuing ahead as another path joins from the right.

❽ After a while, you enter a more lush area of bracken and birch trees. At a fork, go left, then merge with a path from the right. Continue ahead into a clearing, where you will see the Nine Ladies Stone Circle ahead of you. *This enigmatic feature is thought to be 4000 years old, and the name comes from local legend: the nine stones were once ladies, dancing in a circle, before being turned to stone as punishment for dancing on a Sunday. The fiddler who provided their music was also turned to stone – "he" can be seen a short distance away, standing alone in the middle of a grassy path.*

❾ Head to the centre of the circle and look for the Fiddler stone diagonally to your left (it is at 10 o'clock to the angle you have walked from). Take the grassy path past the stone, which becomes more well-defined as you go on. At a fork, keep left. Emerge from the trees and pass the disused New Park Quarry workings on your right. The large Cork Stone will appear ahead of you; continue to reach a junction of paths here.

❿ Turn right, on a path following a fence. Go through a gate and reach a road.

⓫ Turn left on the road and continue for 300m.

Derbyshire & the Peak District

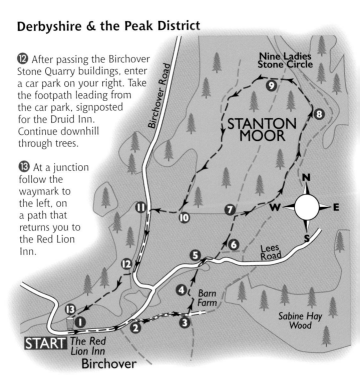

12 After passing the Birchover Stone Quarry buildings, enter a car park on your right. Take the footpath leading from the car park, signposted for the Druid Inn. Continue downhill through trees.

13 At a junction follow the waymark to the left, on a path that returns you to the Red Lion Inn.

OPTIONAL EXTENSION: Instead of returning to the Red Lion Inn at point **13** continue straight on to reach the road by the Druid Inn. Cross the road and take the track to the left of the pub. Just past the buildings, find the entry point to Rowtor Rocks on your right. This is a fantastic area for kids (and big kids!) to explore and scramble around, full of unusual rock formations, carved staircases and secret passages. There is even a 'Druid's Cave'! After your exploration, return to the entrance, turn left on the track, then continue ahead on the main road to the Red Lion Inn.

The Nine Ladies Stone Circle

15 Hartington & Beresford Dale

3 miles (5 km)

Start: Parson's Field Car Park, just outside Hartington village (pay and display, toilets available). **Postcode:** SK17 0BE
Public Transport: The 442 Buxton- Ashbourne bus.
OS Map: OL24 The Peak District: White Peak Area. **Grid Ref:** SK127602.
Terrain: Riverside and fields, on good paths and quiet lanes.
Refreshments: Numerous cafés and pubs are available in Hartington village.

HIGHLIGHTS

With its jumble of honey-coloured houses and cottage gardens, Hartington is one of the prettiest villages in the Peak District. This walk takes you through lush meadows before following the River Dove through the leafy gorge of Beresford Dale. After dipping into Wolfscote Dale, the return is by quiet lanes and farm tracks offering great views.

THE WALK

❶ Exit the car park onto the road and turn left. Almost immediately, you will see Hartington Farm Shop and some public toilets on the right-hand side of the road. Take the path that goes between the farm shop and toilet buildings, signposted 'Dove Dale via Beresford & Wolfscote Dale'. Follow the path through fields.

Derbyshire & the Peak District

2 Continue straight ahead on the footpath as it crosses a farm track and continues into the meadows ahead. Take a moment here to enjoy the view, and the rich selection of wild flowers that bloom in early summer. Then, continue on the well waymarked path as it follows through a series of fields, and dips below the knoll of Pennilow on your left. It's worth noting that there may be cows in these fields.

3 Leave the fields by a gate into woodland. This is Morson Wood, and a plaque commemorates Les Morson, who planted the trees. The path descends gently to lead you beside the River Dove, passing through lush greenery and beneath impressive limestone crags.

4 Cross the footbridge over the River Dove and continue on the path. You are now in Staffordshire, as the river forms the county boundary. At this point, the river widens into a deep pool known as Pike Pool; there is also an impressive limestone stack standing out of the water.

5 The path arrives at a junction with a farm track. To your left is a small footbridge; cross this and turn right on the riverside path through the meadow. You are now safely back in Derbyshire again!

6 Exit the field through a gate and arrive at a junction of paths next to a small footbridge. *At this point Beresford Dale becomes Wolfscote Dale, and the valley now has a very different feel. There are fewer trees, and sheep graze the valley sides. The result is a much sunnier, open feel and the short turf is sprinkled with wild flowers.* Continue straight ahead along the riverside path to enjoy the views of Wolfscote Dale.

7 For a shorter walk, you can turn around and return to the bridge at any point, but to see the best of Wolfscote Dale, continue straight ahead on the riverside path, past several small weirs to a point where a wooden gate crosses the path. Turn around here and retrace your steps to the junction by the footbridge.

8 Returning to the junction by the footbridge, take the path on your right which heads uphill, signposted for Hartington via Staden. Climb gently on this walled path, through trees and into fields, until it reaches a gate at a T-junction with a lane.

9 Go through this gate and turn left on the lane, signposted for Hartington. Follow the lane uphill and around a bend. Ignore the first public footpath on your left, but almost immediately after look for a wooden signpost for Hartington/NCN 549.

10 Turn left on the bridleway here. This lovely, quiet farm track offers panoramic views across Hartington and to the Warslow Moors. Continue for 500m, passing between two field barns before reaching a T-junction with Reynards Lane.

11 Turn left, signposted for Hartington. As you draw level with two barns on the left, turn left on a footpath between them. Head downhill, and look for a footpath crossing the track. Turn right through the gate to re-join your outward route to Hartington.

Thorpe Cloud

16 Dovedale & Thorpe Cloud

2 miles (3 km)

Start: Dovedale car park, just off the road to Ilam. **Postcode:** DE6 2AY.
OS Map: OL24 The Peak District: White Peak Area. **Grid Ref:** SK146509.
Terrain: Grassy paths and tracks for the main circuit, with gradual ascent
and descent; the optional ascent to Thorpe Cloud summit is much
more steep, rocky and uneven. Be aware that limestone can be very
slippery when wet.
Refreshments: The Dovedale Bar and Lounge at The Izaak Walton
Hotel is only a short distance from the Dovedale car park. There is
also usually an ice cream van at the car park.

HIGHLIGHTS

The deep limestone valley of Dovedale is one of the most popular beauty
spots in the Peak District, and with good reason. Towering above the River
Dove is the dramatic pyramidal peak of Thorpe Cloud. An orbit of the hill
from the valley below offers ever-changing views, and a crossing of the
iconic Dovedale stepping stones. There is also an optional ascent to the
summit of the hill for those seeking a bit of extra adventure, and even
better views!

THE WALK

❶ From the car park, take the path to the right of the public toilets,
which leads to a tarmac track beside the River Dove. The scenery here is

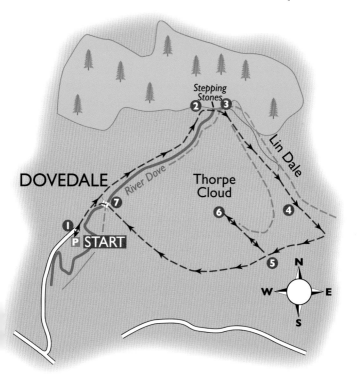

a wonderful contrast between the gently burbling river and the towering rocky crags above. Continue for 500m along the track, to reach the stepping stones across the river.

2 Cross the stepping stones. *Look out for fossilised sea creatures in the limestone blocks as you walk across, a reminder that all this scenery derives from sedimentary rock laid down 360 million years ago, when the area was a tropical sea!*

3 After crossing the river, continue straight ahead on a path. Bear left at

51

a sign, to follow the path marked with blue-topped posts. You are now entering Lin Dale; continue beside the fence and a small stream, and ascend gently up the valley.

❹ At a fork in the path, keep left to continue following the bottom of the valley. When you reach the end of the field, follow the fence around to the right, and re-join the path with the blue marker posts. You can now appreciate the scale of Thorpe Cloud's pyramidal peak as it looms above you.

❺ A marker post with an arrow to the right marks the path up to Thorpe Cloud. Our main route continues straight ahead, but if you wish to make the optional journey to the top, turn right on this path. It is only a short distance to the summit, but the ascent is not for the faint-hearted! It's steep, eroded and involves a bit of scrambling to the vertiginous summit. The views are well worth the effort though, with the River Dove glittering far below you, and Ilam Hall prominent to the west. *The unusual, lumpy summit gives a real mountain-top feel to what is actually quite a small hill. Its knobbly nature is the result of how the hill was formed – this is actually the remains of an ancient coral reef!*

❻ After enjoying the views, carefully retrace your steps back to the main path marker post, and turn right on the path. Follow the marker posts back around the side of the hill, descending to the river.

❼ Cross the river on the footbridge and turn left to return to the car park.

Tissington Hall

17 A Tour of Tissington

2 miles (3 km)

> **Start:** Tissington Car Park (pay and display, toilets available), Darfield Lane. **Postcode:** DE6 1RA.
> **Public Transport:** The 442 Buxton – Ashbourne bus, infrequent.
> **OS Map:** OL24 The Peak District: White Peak Area. **Grid Ref:** SK177520.
> **Terrain:** Easy walking, largely on well-graded tracks and quiet country lanes.
> **Refreshments:** Tissington Snack Kiosk by the car park is open 10–4, seven days a week.

HIGHLIGHTS

The small village of Tissington oozes atmosphere. Nucleated around the historic Tissington Hall, it has a real old English village feel, with cottages, a picturesque church and a village duck pond. It also lends its name to the Tissington Trail, a walking and cycling route on the course of the old Buxton – Ashbourne railway line. This walk takes in part of the trail and the village itself, as well as some delightful meadows and country lanes.

THE WALK

❶ Tissington car park is on the site of the old railway station. Turn left along the trail, signposted 'Tissington Trail to Parsley Hay'. *You are now following the course of the old Buxton – Ashbourne railway line. Primarily serving isolated farm traffic, the railway was never really profitable and closed in the 1950s. Today, the trackbed is managed by the Peak District National Park Authority as a*

53

Derbyshire & the Peak District

popular multi-user trail. Initially in a lush, wooded cutting, the scenery opens up after a short while, and there are great views across the Derbyshire Dales.

2 An old bridge appears ahead of you, spanning the trail. Just before reaching this bridge, look for a signpost on the left, 'To Tissington & Parwich'. Leave the trail on this path, which heads up to a lane.

3 Turn left on the lane, passing Trail Barn and the farm at High Flats. This very quiet farm lane makes for a pleasant wander, especially in early summer when the verges are alive with wild flowers.

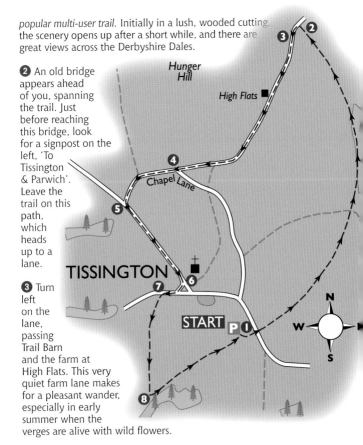

Hunger Hill

High Flats

Chapel Lane

TISSINGTON

START

N
W · E
S

4 The lane bends to the left and passes a small caravan site before arriving at a junction. Continue straight ahead here and pass the sweet shop and café (an ideal place to refuel).

5 Drop down to reach Tissington village, and another road junction. Turn left here, on the main street through the village. *On your right is Tissington Hall, built in 1609 by Francis Fitzherbert, and still in the Fitzherbert family today. The hall opens for visitors several weekends each month in the spring and summer.*

6 Pass the church on your left and shortly afterwards you arrive at The Green, a small grassy area dotted with chestnut trees, and a junction with another road. It's worth having a quick look to your left to see the village duck pond, but our route turns right on the road. Pass the bus shelter, the Yew Tree Well and a candle-making workshop.

7 Immediately after the Yew Tree Well, look for a small wooden gate on the left, next to the candle shop. Go through the gate to enter the field. Follow this path through another field, and soon the old railway embankment carrying the Tissington Trail appears ahead.

8 Leave the field by a gate, and join the trail by the steps on your right. Turn left along the trail; shortly afterwards you will arrive back at the car park.

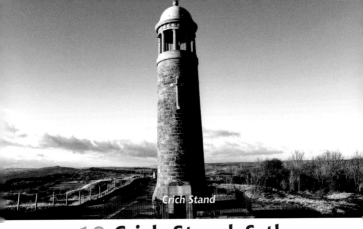

Crich Stand

18 Crich Stand & the Cromford Canal

3¼ miles (5.5 km)
(shorter option possible if you use a tram for part of the route)

Start: The entrance to Crich Tramway Village. Car parking is available for visitors to the museum, or there is street parking in the village. **Postcode:** DE4 5DP.

Public Transport: The 140 & 141 Matlock – Alfreton/Ripley buses. Whatstandwell station is a mile away, on the Derby-Matlock railway. This walk passes the station – join at point 8 to begin from here.

OS Map: OL24 The Peak District: White Peak Area. **Grid Ref:** SK345548.

Terrain: Good paths and tracks through fields and woodland, with ascent and descent. There may be cows in the fields; keep dogs on a lead.

Refreshments: Crich Stand Memorial Café or there are several pubs in Crich.

HIGHLIGHTS

The village of Crich sits high above the Derwent Valley. This walk explores the wooded valley sides and ghosts of old industry, as well as visiting the terrific viewpoint of Crich Stand. Crich is also home to the National Tramway Museum, which you could combine with the walk for a full day out.

THE WALK

1 From the entrance to Crich Tramway Village, turn left on the road, and then left again at a road junction, following a sign for 'Regimental Memorial Tower & Tansley'. Turn left through a gate, to follow a tarmac path running alongside the road.

2 Go through another gate and turn left on the driveway to the memorial grounds. Pass a tearoom and enter the memorial area, dedicated to the Sherwood Foresters regiment. Continue straight ahead to reach Crich Memorial Tower, which can be accessed for a small donation. *The tower is a replica lighthouse, complete with working light! Climbing the spiral steps brings you to a balustrade overlooking the valleys of the Derwent and Amber.*

3 Look for a path running to the right of the tower, signposted to 'Glory Mine'. Follow this path around the edge of

Derbyshire & the Peak District

the huge disused quarry below, which is slowly returning to nature, then descend gently to reach the end of the Crich tramline. If you have purchased a ticket for the tram museum, you could catch a tram back to Crich from here, or if not you can watch the trams come and go for a while.

❹ Cross the tracks and follow the footpath downhill through trees to reach a farm. Continue straight ahead on the farm driveway to reach a road.

❺ Cross the road, turn right and then immediately take a footpath on your left. Follow the path downhill through fields, beside a stream and into woodland.

❻ Keep left at a junction of paths. Continue through woodland and mossy, disused quarries until you reach a road. Cross the road and, following a signpost for 'Cromford Canal', continue downhill. The path bends to the left as you reach the canal; shortly afterwards cross the canal on a footbridge.

❼ Turn left on the canal towpath, signposted to Ambergate. After 300m, follow the canal under a roadbridge. Shortly, a footbridge spans the canal.

❽ Use the footbridge to cross the canal and follow the path to meet a road.

❾ Turn right on the road, and just after a school, turn left on Hindersitch Lane. This quiet lane heads uphill through Crich Carr village. Just after passing a chapel, turn right at a fork in front of a small, triangular building. Follow this narrow lane to meet Glen Road and turn right. Climb through pretty cottages, continuing as the road narrows to become a footpath.

❿ Meeting another lane, turn right, past a pretty row of cottages, then turn left on a stone-stepped path behind the cottages – signposted 'Derwent Valley Walk'. Climb through trees and emerge into a field.

⓫ Continue straight ahead, passing through a gap in a wall, to the left of some trees. Continue through a series of fields; the climb has now levelled out and there are great views. After cresting the hill, meet a junction of paths. Turn left on a footpath and continue to meet a road.

⓬ Turn right on the road to return to the Tramway Village.

Mapperley Reservoir

19 Shipley Country Park

2½ miles (4 km)

Start: Mapperley Reservoir Car Park (pay & display, access via Mapperley village only). **Postcode:** DE7 6BR.
OS Map: Explorer 269 Chesterfield & Alfreton. **Grid Ref:** SK434436.
Terrain: Good paths, tracks and quiet lanes through meadows and woodland, with gentle ascent and descent.
Refreshments: Derby Lodge Tearooms is at the centre of the country park. There are also pubs in Mapperley.

HIGHLIGHTS

The area around Heanor and Ilkeston was once an important coal-mining area, but since the collapse of the industry it has been returning to nature. Shipley Country Park is one of the hidden gems of the area. Centred on the site of the long-demolished Shipley Hall, it is now a pleasant mosaic of woods, meadows and water with plenty of historical interest. This figure-of-eight loop showcases the variety of the country park.

THE WALK

❶ Once parked, head to the vehicle entrance of the car park at Mapperley Reservoir. Turn left and follow Shipley Lane uphill. This quiet country lane is closed to vehicles, and makes for a pleasant walk as it rises gently through rolling fields.

2 As you reach the crest of the hill, pass some buildings on your right. These are some of the surviving outbuildings of the Shipley Hall estate; of particular note is a brick water tower. Continue on the lane as it begins to descend, and shortly afterwards you will reach Derby Lodge Tearooms on your right.

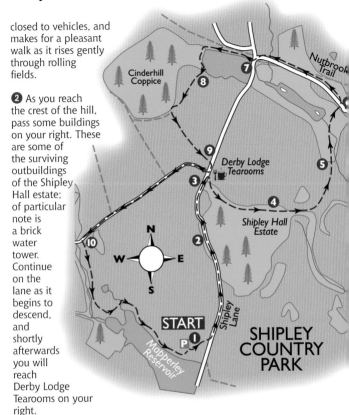

3 Take the track that leaves Shipley Lane to the right, immediately after the lodge. Follow this into the wooded grounds of the Shipley Hall estate.

4 Shortly afterwards, you arrive at a junction of tracks. Keep on the furthest left track, which runs beside the boundary wall of the former hall grounds. Pass Nottingham Lodge on your right, and continue on the track to the bottom of the hill. Continue straight ahead, into trees, and pass a vehicle barrier.

5 Keep straight on as the lane begins to climb through the woods. Just after passing Coppice House, you arrive at a junction of roads and paths.

6 Turn left, taking the bridleway which runs next to a lane. This is part of the Nutbrook Trail, which follows the course of an old railway line – one of the reminders of this area's industrial past. The trail crosses a lane and then draws level with Osborne's Pond, a former colliery pond now returned to nature.

7 Leave the Nutbrook Trail here on a path to the left, then turn right on a path along the edge of the water. Continue to the end of Osborne's Pond, then keep left to go through a gap in the fence. Follow the path around the head of the pond. Just before reaching the far side of the pond take a path to the right, heading slightly uphill.

8 Skirting Cinderhill Coppice, the path climbs gently. Just before the summit of the rise, you reach a junction of paths. Turn left to go through a gap in the hedge and head straight across a meadow on a mown path. This area is a blaze of colour in spring and early summer, full of colourful wild flowers like hawkweed, clover and yellow rattle. Ignore other mown paths to both sides and continue straight ahead to reach Shipley Lane.

9 Turn right on Shipley Lane, to find yourself back at Derby Lodge Tearooms crossroads; here's your chance for a second cup of tea if needed! Our walk takes the lane to the right, which heads downhill between hedges. Ignore all turnings on the right, and reach the bottom of the hill.

10 Turn left on a bridleway beside a gate, signposted for Mapperley Reservoir. This wide path then heads into John Wood, carpeted with bluebells in spring. Just after emerging from trees, a path appears from the right. Turn left on this path, which initially runs parallel to the bridleway, before following the edge of Mapperley Reservoir. Look out for dragonflies and damselflies in summer, and keep on the waterside path until you see steps on your left. These lead you back to the car park.

20 Calke

2½ miles (4 km)

Start: Severn Trent Round Car Park, Calke. Alternatively park at the National Trust car park at Calke Abbey and start the walk from point 8. **Postcode:** DE73 7LD.
OS Map: Explorer 245 The National Forest. **Grid Ref:** SK374226.
Terrain: Good paths and tracks through parkland and woods; gently undulating.
Refreshments: Calke Abbey Stableyard café & restaurant (National Trust).

HIGHLIGHTS

The Calke Estate is a fascinating place, with paths winding through lush woodland, tranquil ponds and grassy meadows. This walk offers a tour through the varied landscapes of the park, passing Calke Abbey, and an amazing historic tree!

THE WALK

❶ Leave the car park by the main entrance. Take the path immediately on your right, through a gap in the wall. Continue to the shore of Staunton Harold Reservoir, and follow along the water's edge for 250m to the weir at the end of the reservoir.

2 Cross the bridge over the weir, passing a pond. Continue as the path climbs gently and crosses a reservoir access track, before reaching the top of the hill and curving to the left. Look out for deer grazing in the parkland as you continue along the path to a gate.

3 Go through the gate to arrive at a junction of paths. Turn left, heading downhill through the woodland. Ignore the first path on the right, but just before the bottom of the hill turn right on another path leading up steps and into the trees.

4 Continue on this path through woodland before emerging into open parkland. The grass and wild flowers are allowed to grow long here, creating lush meadows for bees and butterflies. Heading into more trees, look out for a huge, veteran oak on your right: 'The Old Man of Calke'. *This amazing, gnarled tree is thought to be almost 1200 years old. To put things into perspective, it was growing in this spot about two hundred years before the Battle of Hastings!* Having paid your respects to the Old Man, continue out of the trees and pass through a gate.

5 Just after the gate, keep left at a junction of paths, following the pink waymarkers. This path descends gently, before joining another path from the right. The peaceful body of water beside the path is Betty's Pond, covered with waterlilies in summer. If you are very lucky, you may also spot the electric blue flash of a kingfisher.

6 Just after Betty's Pond, the path arrives at a fence with two gates. Take the gate on the left, waymarked 'National Forest Way'. Immediately after, take another path on the left, following blue and pink waymarks up steps; this path continues along a grassy bank.

7 At a fork, keep left to drop down to Mere Pond. Enjoy more peaceful waterside views as you walk beside the pond, before reaching another path junction. Turn sharp right, and head up steps to reach the National Trust car park at Calke Abbey.

8 Go straight ahead, through the car park and into the welcome area around the Stableyard. There are toilets, a café and shop here. To continue on the walk, follow the wide path on the right of the Stableyard buildings.

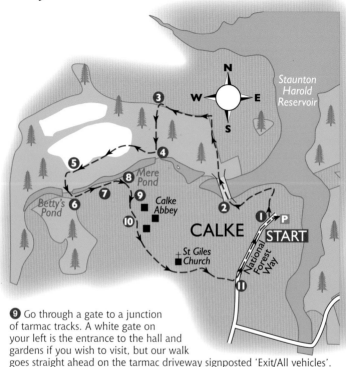

9 Go through a gate to a junction of tarmac tracks. A white gate on your left is the entrance to the hall and gardens if you wish to visit, but our walk goes straight ahead on the tarmac driveway signposted 'Exit/All vehicles'.

10 Keep beside the driveway and descend to a spot with great views of Calke Abbey. *There is no longer an abbey here, but the current building was built on the site of a medieval religious house. The 17th-century house remained in the Harpur-Crewe family until 1985, but is now a National Trust property. It is unique in being presented unrestored, a time capsule of the decline of the landed gentry.* Continue past the church of St Giles, then keep on the path beside the drive as it goes through a gate and into trees before arriving at a junction.

11 Turn left on the lane to return to the car park.